Good Grief

Keeping God Your Focus in Trials

Heather Jones

KAIO PUBLICATIONS, INC.

Good Grief: Keeping God Your Focus In Trials

Published by Kaio Publications
http://kaiopublications.org

Printed and Bound in the
United States of America
All Rights Reserved

ISBN: 978-1-952955-10-5

Edited by Gary Pollard
Cover & Layout design by Lee Snow

"*Good Grief* is a much-needed addition to any Christian's library. Good material has been absent on processing grief as a Christian; it is an uncomfortable subject many people tend to gloss over. Heather deals with this delicate subject compassionately and poignantly, pointing her readers straight to Scripture. Not only does this book do a fantastic job of walking through the issue of grief, but Heather also helps build good Bible study habits along the way. I see this as an excellent aid for dealing with personal grief, an evangelistic tool, and a resource to help comfort the church's grieving."

- **Kristy Huntsman**, *editor-in-chief at Come Fill Your Cup and author of several books in the Finer Grounds series*

"It's not often you run across a book that applies to everyone. Loss, sorrow, discouragement, disappointment...we've all experienced some pain regardless of age or circumstance. Heather Jones has an easygoing writing style, and she engages the reader through this very practical study. Her goal is to "lead your mind in your trial instead of your trial leading you." *Good Grief* is your personal journal of discovery and strength-building, a coping tool to promote healing and peace through hardship. I have a feeling this will be the book I send to friends and loved ones who are hurting."

- **Kathy Pollard**, *author of Return to Me: What to Do When Loved Ones Fall Away*

Seek God's wisdom in trials and you'll overcome everything else.

Why Grief?

Grief is something we're all going to go through at some point, and we won't always expect it. Grief is found in more areas than just death. It's pain from divorce, death of a loved pet, traumatic events and so much more. Grief can be defined as a deep sorrow. For me, grief entered my life in several different ways in my walk with Christ. My first experiences with grief happened long before I knew Christ. In middle school my parents got a divorce and in high school I lost family members in a short period of time. In college I lost a lot of friends to drinking and driving. It was a time in life I didn't know I could go to a loving God for help, so it was really hard to work out the pieces of my heartache. I also didn't know anything about grief. I didn't understand the process or that it was even okay to grieve or that it was even okay to grieve when they weren't even my family.

Since then, I experienced the grief of a miscarriage at nine weeks pregnant. I didn't even get a break before another major tragedy hit. Fortunately, this happened when my faith was stronger than ever. I knew God and how much love He has when we trust Him with our heartaches. I lost someone very close to me: my brother. He passed in a sudden, tragic incident. It's still just as fresh to me two years later. I vividly remember how I felt when I found out. The weeks that followed and the aftermath is still so fresh to me. I had to stay connected with God and find some way to keep my faith while overwhelmed with grief.

I wrote this book to show others how to survive even the most devastating grief. There are all kinds of resources to help someone manage grief, but only one that can truly satisfy the soul. God's wisdom helped me to overcome grief. His wisdom gave me peace and hope when I needed it the most.

If you're going through hard times, I believe this book will help you find comfort in our loving Father. It certainly helped me! In the end you will come out stronger. I pray that God's wisdom will help each of you!

In His Service,

Heather Jones

Getting Started

You'll want to have some supplies handy for all of the weekly studies.

- Bible
- Colored pens for color coding different sections of the text, underlining, and boxing
- Colored pencils for key wording passages

If you have never broken down a Bible passage, this is an example of the steps I go through to dissect a writer's message.

- Step 1: Read the passage. Find out who wrote it. What significant events took place when it was written? Why was it written to begin with? Note: Some of these questions are unknown in the Psalms.
- Step 2: Find keywords (significant words repeated throughout the text).
- Step 3: Find repeated phrases.
- Step 4: Are there any lists?
- Step 5: Are there any contrasts or comparisons?
- Step 6: Is there an obvious outline in the passage?
- Step 7: What point is the author trying to make?
- Step 8: How does this apply to your life?

One or more of these steps may not apply to every passage. The passage may not have lists or contrasts or comparisons, for example.

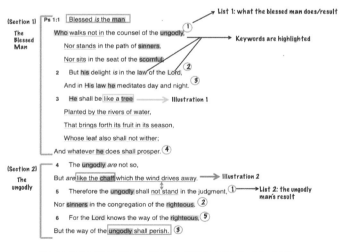

Psalm 1 (NKJV)
Step 1

Read the passage and notice the differences between an unrighteous man and a godly man.

Step 2

Keywords Found:
- Lord/His (yellow)
- Law (blue)
- Blessed Man References (green): Man, Who, His, He, Tree, Righteous
- Ungodly Man References (red): Ungodly, Sinners, Scornful, Chaff

Step 3

There are no repeated phrases in this text.

Step 4

There are two lists in Psalm 1:

The Blessed Man

1. Does not walk in the counsel of the ungodly, nor stand in their path, nor sit in the seat of the scornful.
2. He finds delight in the law of the Lord.
3. He meditates on the law day and night.
4. Whatever he does he prospers in.
5. The Lord knows the righteous, blessed man.

The Ungodly Man

1. The ungodly will not stand in the judgement.
2. Not in fellowship with the righteous.
3. The ungodly will perish.

Step 5

- The blessed man is compared to a tree that brings fruit in its season and contrasted with the ungodly man where the Lord only knows the righteous but not the ungodly.
- The ungodly man is compared to chaff being blown around in the wind because he will not be able to stand in judgement.

Step 6

- Section 1: The Blessed Man
- Section 2: The Ungodly Man

Step 7

There are two choices we can make in this life. We can choose to be righteous, or we can take the path of the ungodly.

Step 8

This message applies to us today. We have to decide which path we want to take. Either to be righteous or to be ungodly.

Surrendering Thoughts

The passage breakdowns will be done a little piece at a time each day of the week. They are such a fun and rewarding way to study your Bible. This method can be used in small sections of text or with whole books or chapters.

There will also be a section called "Surrendering Thoughts." What does this mean and how do you do that? You can use this section as a space for confession or getting thoughts off your mind that may be weighing you down." This is a great place to do that. It was a little awkward at first to open up to myself and to God about these struggles, but over time it gets easier. You will notice a change in the thoughts you've surrendered when you look back at them weeks or months later. When I lost my brother, I started writing questions to him. It turned into writing notes about memories we had together so I'd always remember them.

Week One
Day One

"Consider it all joy my brethren, when you encounter various trials, knowing that the testing of your faith produces endurance."
- James 1:2, 3

Starting in James 1:1, we first see that James was a bondservant of God and the Lord Jesus Christ. A bondservant is a voluntary slave, willing to do whatever it takes to make the truth known about who Jesus is and stay committed to working for Him. James the Lord's brother was a late bloomer in following Jesus. He didn't become a follower until after the resurrection, but he became a great worker and servant for the church. In this letter to the twelve tribes who were dispersed abroad because of persecution (Acts 8) he helps them to overcome their trials.

Can you say that you're a voluntary slave of Christ? If not, why not?
_____
_____
_____
_____
_____

James 1:2, "Consider it all joy my brethren, when you encounter various trials."

The word "consider" in this verse means "to lead." What James is saying to us is that we need to lead our minds to joy when we face various trials. I never thought in our age we really faced anything like the trials and persecution they faced in the first century. In reality our trials are what cause our suffering and grief. These trials can be from financial issues, death of a family member or friend, miscarriage, marriage issues, and so many other unexpected changes. There are practical ways to lead your mind in trials.

- You can start by spending time in prayer about the sudden pain felt in the situation. Pray for your family and friends that are also

affected by the trial. Pray for your heart to find peace through God.
- Then find someone else to help! Help someone in a worse condition than you are in and you will start to find hope again and a purpose to keep going.
- Spend time learning more of God's Word and grow your relationship with Him. This is the most important thing you can do right now because He is the only one who will bring you out of the suffering.

Are there any other ways that you can lead your mind in your trial instead of your trial leading you?

_____
_____
_____
_____

James 1:3, 4 "...knowing that the testing of your faith produces endurance. And let endurance have its perfect result, so that you may be perfect and complete, lacking in nothing."

The word "know" here in Greek is the word ginosko, an "experiential knowledge." These trials are a test of our faith. In these trials, we have the choice to learn from them and get stronger or let our faith fail and let Satan win. If we are constantly growing through our trials and keeping our eyes focused on God, He will pull us through the trial and every trial to come. When we are made perfect we are made mature in our faith, which is the result of our endurance.

James 1:5, "But if any of you lacks wisdom, let him ask of God, who gives to all generously and without reproach and it will be given to him."

In verse 4, we found that when we endure through our trials we can be made perfect or whole. In verse 5, "if any of you lacks wisdom," means if we are not perfect or whole yet we should ask God to give us wisdom. There are three things listed in this verse that we know God does for us: 1. God gives wisdom to all. 2. He gives generously and 3. He gives without reproach.

What is this wisdom? Wisdom is seeing earthly things the way God sees them. When you ask God to give you wisdom during a trial, think about what you are asking. Go to God in humility and ask Him to give you strength and knowledge to get through the trial and help others around you. Ask God to help you know what to say when your heart is hurting. We sometimes ask the wrong things (like, "remove the trial from me"), but we should be asking to be taught by the trial.

James 1:6, "But he must ask in faith, without doubting, for the one who doubts is like the surf of the sea, driven and tossed by the wind."

Let's talk about what faith is for a second. Faith can be translated as trust. Faith is trusting in the invisible working power of God. When we doubt, we are ultimately trying to judge between two things. If you're a person who becomes driven and tossed by the wind, then you have lost sight of who you're trusting in. Therefore, when we lack wisdom and are asking God for help in this trial, we need to make sure we fully trust He is going provide for us.

James 1:7-10, "For that man ought not to expect anything from the Lord, being a double-minded man, unstable in all his ways. But the brother of humble circumstances is to glory in his high position; and the rich man is to glory in his humiliation, because like flowering grass he will pass away."

That man shouldn't expect anything from the lord because he has no faith. He asked in doubting, so he is a double-minded man and unstable. You cannot serve two masters. If your faith is unstable the foundation will fall! How can God give us an answer when we aren't fully trusting in Him? If the answer was no, would we lose our perspective? The rich man trusted in his wealth but to his humiliation it will pass away, and so will he. James is saying to trust God and realize that your trust is being tested.

GOD DOESN'T PROMISE TO FIX CONDITIONS, BUT TO HELP YOU TO FIND WISDOM THROUGH THE CONDITION.

Are you trusting God more than yourself and others around you right now? If so, what are some ways you are trusting God through your trial and suffering?

What kind of wisdom are you asking God to give you?

Make a list of people you may know who have been through a similar trial. Make it a goal to reach out to them for comfort, and if they are strong Christians ask for advice on how they got through it.

Grief Facts from Dr. H. Norman Wright:

There are phases to a crisis. These phases include the initial impact, withdrawal and confusion, adjustment, and reconstruction and reconciliation.

The first phase is the impact of the crisis. This phase is often called the fight or flight pattern because you have to make a decision to fight the problem to find resolution or run away and ignore the problem.

In this first phase there are feelings of being numb, guilt and searching for a lost object or person through photos or replacing an object. Feelings should not be denied or hidden, or it will only make the process of finding resolution longer. (Wright, pg. 143)

Thoughts to Surrender

Prayer for Yourself

Day Two

For the next few days, the goal is to meditate on one passage and find something new from it each time you read it. Today, read through and look for words that are found more than once. These are significant to the text, such as Lord, seek, ask, me, my, you, etc. Feel free to color these words with colored pencils or put boxes around them.

When we keyword a text, it helps identify changes in the writer's focus, like a thought change or a different person being introduced.

Psalm 27:4-8 (NASB), "One thing I have asked from the Lord, that I shall seek: that I may dwell in the house of the Lord all the days of my life, to behold the beauty of the Lord and to meditate in His temple. For in the day of trouble He will conceal me in His tabernacle; in the secret place of His tent He will hide me; He will lift me up on a rock. And now my head will be lifted up above my enemies around me, and I will offer in His tent sacrifices with shouts of joy; I will sing, yes, I will sing praises to the Lord. Hear, O Lord, when I cry with my voice, and be gracious to me and answer me. When You said, "Seek My face," my heart said to You, "Your face, O Lord, I shall seek."

"Trust in Him at all times, O people; pour out your heart before Him; God is a refuge for you." - Psalm 62:8

Thoughts to Surrender

Prayer for Yourself

Day Three

Today, go back to our text in Psalm 27 and read it again. This time look for any connecting thoughts or phrases throughout. I usually underline these and draw arrows to each other.

Example of what I found: He starts and ends each section with, "I shall seek."

What are some connections you found?

Thoughts to Surrender

Prayer for Yourself

Day Four

We are still in our text of Psalm 27. We are going to re-read this text every day and pull something new out of it. Yesterday you looked for connecting thoughts and phrases. Today, look for contrasts or comparisons with those connecting thoughts. I usually draw arrows to each other.

What are some contrasts or comparisons you found?

Thoughts to Surrender

Prayer for Yourself

Day Five

Today in Psalm 27 we are going to make observations. Was this a prayer? What was the writer praying for? Why did he ask for that? What was his attitude throughout the prayer?

Are there any other observations you can make?

Thoughts to Surrender

Prayer for Yourself

Day Six

This is the last day we will be in Psalm 27! Read it one more time. I'm sure you have it memorized by now. Make application to your own life from the observations and characteristics of the writer and his prayer.

"I love you, O Lord, my strength. The Lord is my rock and my fortress and my deliverer, my God, my rock, in whom I take refuge; my shield and the horn of my salvation, my stronghold." - Psalm 18:1, 2

Thoughts to Surrender

Prayer for Yourself

Day Seven

Find a quote that you really like or has stuck out to you lately. It can be encouraging, inspirational, spiritual, anything that you need at this time. Write the quote here and if you're artsy, have fun with it!

Thoughts to Surrender

Prayer for Yourself

"And our hope for you is firmly grounded, knowing that as you are sharers of our sufferings, so also you are sharers of our comfort." - 2 Corinthians 1:7

For this lesson we will be in 2 Corinthians 1:3-7. Let's look at a few things about 2 Corinthians before we get started. We learn more about Paul from this book than from any other book. We see more of his personal feelings in this book than any other book in the New Testament. Paul wrote this letter because there were false teachers in Corinth that were trying to corrupt everything he had taught them. They attempted to tear down Paul's character with the people of Corinth in order to win them over. Paul starts by speaking about suffering because he knows what it's like to suffer.

In the section of text, I want you to go through and color or highlight the word **"comfort"** and in another color highlight every time you see the word "suffering", "affliction" or "tribulation" depending on your translation. Based on your colors you can tell that this passage is broken down into two themes: **comfort** and suffering. Now that we have that in mind and on paper let's get started!

2 Cor. 1:3,4 "Blessed be the God and Father of our Lord Jesus Christ, the Father of mercies and God of all comfort, who comforts us in all our affliction so that we will be able to comfort those who are in any affliction with the comfort with which we ourselves are comforted by God."

Paul is speaking from experience, which can be found down in verse 8 where he mentions his trouble in Asia. The details of this affliction are found in 1 Corinthians 15:30-32. Paul thought he was going to die at this time, but he found comfort in God through this affliction and all other sufferings he'd endured.

We often hear women say that they have comfort foods they binge eat when they've had a bad day or are stressed or going through hard times. Then there are women who turn to "shopping therapy" and before they know it they own more mugs than cabinets or more shoes than closet space. Don't get me wrong, these things aren't necessarily wrong unless you go broke shopping. These are ways we cope physically or keep our minds occupied, right?

What are things you find comfort in during the hard times?
_____
_____
_____
_____

Finding spiritual comfort is what's most important.. Paul had comfort because he trusted in God so much. He had assurance of hope no matter what happened in his situation. The way God works to comfort us in our afflictions is through the endurance and progress of our faith (1 Thess. 3:2,3,6,7). We looked at endurance that makes us mature in our faith in our first lesson from James 1.

With that comfort, we can help others who have experienced similar tragedies as ourselves. We have sought the wisdom of God like Paul did to obtain this comfort. Maybe you found comfort in God while going through a divorce, death of a loved one, or any of life's trials. If you know someone who needs that same comfort, share it with them! Share God's wisdom with them.

You can sympathize with people who are hurting the same way you have. You can pray with them. You can spend time with them so they know they are not alone.

Do you know anyone who has been through the same trial you experienced and came out with a stronger faith?
_____
_____
_____

2 Cor. 1:5,6 "For just as the sufferings of Christ are ours in abundance, so also our comfort is abundant through Christ. But if we are afflicted, it is for your comfort and salvation; or if we are comforted, it is for your comfort, which is effective in the patient enduring of the same sufferings which we also suffer…"

Paul described the suffering we experience in our Christian walk as being an extension of Christ's suffering. When you know the power of Christ and His resurrection then you know the fellowship of his suffering and are conformed to His death (Phil 3:10). When the body of Christ suffers, Christ also suffers. In Romans 8:17, when Christians suffer with Christ we expect to be glorified with Christ. We can receive this comfort from God when we remain faithful in our suffering.

In verse 6, the "we" Paul is talking about includes himself and others preaching to them. They received most of their affliction for preaching Christ, and their faithfulness despite persecution helped save many souls. When others saw their example, it gave them hope.

When we remain faithful through suffering we have that assurance and expectation of being glorified with Christ. So, keep seeking wisdom from God, pray, and don't lose the hope that is before you.

2 Cor. 1:7 "and our hope for you is firmly grounded, knowing that as you are sharers of our sufferings, so also you are sharers of our comfort."

We suffer together and comfort together as Christians. Take comfort from your fellow Christians and let them help lift you up in your affliction. It's not easy to be open about our pain, but it helps us get rid of the burdens on our heart. We have to lift those burdens if we want to keep going and grow closer to God.

KEEP SEEKING WISDOM AND SET YOUR SIGHTS ON BEING GLORIFIED WITH CHRIST!

What are some burdens on your heart that you need to open up to someone about?

What happens when we remain faithful to God and choose not to doubt Him in our suffering?

What are some ways you can personally find comfort in God? What are some things you can do to help yourself right now?

Grief Facts from Dr. H. Norman Wright:

The second phase of crisis and grief can be known as withdrawal and confusion. This can happen days to weeks after the crisis has already occurred.

In this phase there is a tendency to deny the feelings more than in other stages. There can be a rise of intensified feelings and anger. The support from friends and family is needed during this time to allow feelings to be expressed. (Wright, pg. 147)

Thoughts to Surrender

_____

_____

_____

_____

_____

_____

_____

_____

_____

_____

_____

_____

_____

_____

_____

_____

_____

_____

_____

Prayer for Others

Day Two

It's a new week and a new passage! For the next few days the goal is to meditate on one passage and find something new each time you read it. Today, read through and look for words that are found more than once and are significant to the text, such as Lord, praise, work, righteous, me, my, you, etc. Feel free to color these words with colored pencils or put boxes around them.

Psalm 145 (NASB), "I will extol You, my God, O King, And I will bless Your name forever and ever. Every day I will bless You, And I will praise Your name forever and ever. Great is the Lord, and highly to be praised, And His greatness is unsearchable. One generation shall praise Your works to another, And shall declare Your mighty acts. On the glorious splendor of Your majesty And on Your wonderful works, I will meditate. Men shall speak of the power of Your awesome acts, And I will tell of Your greatness. They shall eagerly utter the memory of Your abundant goodness And will shout joyfully of Your righteousness. The Lord is gracious and merciful; Slow to anger and great in lovingkindness. The Lord is good to all, And His mercies are over all His works. All Your works shall give thanks to You, O Lord, And Your godly ones shall bless You. They shall speak of the glory of Your kingdom And talk of Your power; To make known to the sons of men Your mighty acts And the glory of the majesty of Your kingdom. Your kingdom is an everlasting kingdom, And Your dominion endures throughout all generations. The Lord sustains all who fall And raises up all who are bowed down. The eyes of all look to You, And You give them their food in due time. You open Your hand And satisfy the desire of every living thing. The Lord is righteous in all His ways And kind in all His deeds. The Lord is near to all who call upon Him, To all who call upon Him in truth. He will fulfill the desire of those who fear Him; He will also hear their cry and will save them. The Lord keeps all who love Him, But all the wicked He will destroy. My mouth will speak the praise of the Lord, And all flesh will bless His holy name forever and ever.

What are your observations from the text so far? How many of each recurring word did you find? Any patterns?

"Surely the righteous will give thanks to Your name; The upright will dwell in Your presence." - Psalm 140:13

Thoughts to Surrender

Prayer for Yourself

Day Three

Read Psalm 145 again. This time look for any distinct breaks in the text. Is there at a point where the focus changes from self to the Lord? Put a big bracket at each section you found.

What are some breaks in the text you found?

Thoughts to Surrender

Prayer for Others

_____

_____

_____

_____

_____

_____

_____

_____

_____

_____

_____

_____

_____

_____

_____

_____

_____

_____

_____

_____

_____

_____

_____

_____

_____

_____

_____

Day Four

We are still in our text of Psalm 145. Yesterday we looked for different sections or breaks in the text. Today, look for contrasts or comparisons in the sections you found. I usually draw arrows to each other.

What are some contrasts or comparisons you found?

"Worthy are You, our Lord and our God, to receive glory and honor and power; for You created all things, and because of Your will they existed, and were created." - Revelation 4:11

Thoughts to Surrender

Prayer for Yourself

Day Five

Today in Psalm 145 we are going to make observations. There are a lot of, "the Lord is," statements throughout the passage. Make a list of all of these.

Are there any other observations you can make?

Thoughts to Surrender

Prayer for Others

Day Six

This is the last day in Psalm 145! Read it one more time. Make application to your own life from the observations and characteristics of the writer. Did you notice things that you could start adding to your prayer life?

What are the differences between your own prayers and the praise of David? What do you want to start adding to your prayers to grow closer to God?

"Glory in His holy name; Let the heart of those who seek the Lord be glad. Seek the Lord and His strength; Seek His face continually."
- Psalm 105:3,4

Thoughts to Surrender

Prayer for Yourself

Day Seven

Find a quote that you really like or has stuck out to you lately. It can be encouraging, inspirational, spiritual, anything that you need at this time. Write the quote here and if you're artsy, have fun with it!

Thoughts to Surrender

Prayer for Others

Week Three
Day One

**"And to man He said, 'Behold, the fear of the Lord, that is wisdom; And to depart from evil is understanding."
- Job 28:28**

We have looked at wisdom for two weeks now, and we're going to look at it some more this week. Why? Because when we are suffering we tend to forget to seek wisdom, not from other people but from God. Sometimes it's easier to run to a best friend, a family member or someone else to help you in these times. I'm here to tell you that they do not have the wisdom that God does. They can provide comfort, but God and His Word contain more comfort and peace than any pep talk ever could and I know from firsthand experience.

We're often told that the book of Job is all about suffering. It's also typically the first book we turn to when it comes to suffering. While both are true, there is a deeper message in the book of Job that I feel gets overlooked: wisdom. I do suggest you take the time to read the whole book of Job because there are so many great details about his suffering. How he responded to each trial is a great example for us today.

Specifically, I want to spend some time looking at Job 28. Chapter 28 is a continued response from Job rebuking his friend Bildad in Job 26:1.

This week I want you to dig a little deeper for our lesson. After you've read Job 28 color all of the keywords in the text. This helps you get a clear vision of any breaks in the text or change of topic.

What are some of the words you found?
_____
_____
_____

Now let's try to break up the text to see if there are any topic changes. You can section the text out with brackets if you'd like to have a visual. I look for questions, or man's actions versus God's.

Now that you've taken the time to really look at the text, let's make some connections.

In the first section of text you might have noticed how man takes the time to really search for the treasures of the earth. Only man can find these treasures and he goes to great lengths to unearth them and bring them to the light. We see how man is a hard worker, and intelligent to be able to find these unseen things. It's so interesting that the text even says birds, beasts, and lions can't find this treasure. Only man has that ability! Only man can find these treasures of the earth.

Then there is a shift in our text from the things man can do, to asking the questions in verses 12 and 20, "Where can wisdom be found? And where is this place of understanding?"

Before, it sounded like man had a great deal of wisdom to be able to search out and find these buried treasures. To their dismay, they really lack the most important thing of all time: wisdom. They don't know the value of wisdom because they can't find it.

Wisdom is the most valuable thing of all and is incomparable to anything on earth. You cannot buy it or trade for it, you cannot exchange anything for it. Men spend more time searching for material things. In verses 13 and 22, "it's not found in the living or the dead." This is not something man already has, so they are unaware of it.

If we see the text as being a continued rebuke of Bildad, then it's easy to see the real problem. They (Job's friends) think they have wisdom, but they don't. Job's friends spent a great deal of time trying to figure out what he could have done wrong, since he was a righteous man(Job 1). Who knows why these things happened? In verse 23, God has the answer. In verses 24-27 God says that He is all-knowing.

His point is that they could not possibly know why this happened to such a good person. God knows the answer and knows everything, so they needed to trust God, not themselves. It's never about God giving

Job an answer to his suffering. The same goes for us with our suffering. We tend to ask God, "Why?" more than we take the time to let our faith work. God never promises an answer as to why we're suffering but does require us to trust Him.

The beauty of Job is how he shows us that we need to really trust God when we're suffering. God can use our suffering for good if we let Him. We have to have an open heart so we can see the light in God's Word. Then we can use it to help those around us who need us more than we know.

Job 28:28 is what the whole book of Job is about. "Behold, the fear of the Lord, that is wisdom; And to depart from evil is understanding."

To fear the Lord is to have reverence and submission to Him and to His will. He is our creator and our loving Father who really loves us and wants us to love and respect Him, but that's up to us. We have free will to go to Him. Make the choice to fear Him and run from evil. He has the wisdom we need, whether we're going through a trial or not.

Grief Facts from Dr. H. Norman Wright:

The third phase of a crisis is the adjustment.

This is the [sic] period that may last longer than the other phases. Depression may lessen with a heightened sense of hopefulness for the future. If it's a divorce or loss of a spouse it's recommended in this time to wait at least a year before dating again. This allows for recovery. (Wright, pg. 154)

Thoughts to Surrender

Prayer for Yourself

Day Two

It's a new week and a new passage! For the next few days the goal is to meditate on one passage and find something new each time you read it. Today, read through and look for words that are found more than once and significant to the text such as Lord, God, word, praise, trust, I, me, my, you, they, man, etc. When the words are referring to the same person or people I keep them the same color.

"Be gracious to me, O God, for man has trampled upon me; Fighting all day long he oppresses me. My foes have trampled upon me all day long, For they are many who fight proudly against me. When I am afraid, I will put my trust in You. In God, whose word I praise, In God I have put my trust; I shall not be afraid. What can mere man do to me? All day long they distort my words; All their thoughts are against me for evil. They attack, they lurk, They watch my steps, As they have waited to take my life. Because of wickedness, cast them forth, In anger put down the peoples, O God! You have taken account of my wanderings; Put my tears in Your bottle. Are they not in Your book? Then my enemies will turn back in the day when I call; This I know, that God is for me. In God, whose word I praise, In the Lord, whose word I praise, In God I have put my trust, I shall not be afraid. What can man do to me? Your vows are binding upon me, O God; I will render thank offerings to You. For You have delivered my soul from death, Indeed my feet from stumbling, So that I may walk before God In the light of the living." - Psalm 56

What are your observations from the text so far? How many of each recurring word did you find? Any patterns?

"I will praise the name of God with song, and magnify Him with thanksgiving." - Psalm 69:30

Thoughts to Surrender

Prayer for Others

Day Three

Read Psalm 56 again. This time look for any distinct breaks in the text. Is there at a point where the focus changes from the enemy to the Lord? Put a big bracket at each section you found. This will be easy to see if you colored or put boxes around those words.

What are some breaks in the text you found?

"O God, You are my God; I shall seek You earnestly; My soul thirsts for You, my flesh yearns for You, In a dry and weary land where there is no water." - Psalm 63:1

Thoughts to Surrender

Prayer for Yourself

Day Four

We are still in our text of Psalm 56. Every day we are going to re-read this text and pull something new out of it. Yesterday you looked for different sections or breaks in the text. Today look for any repeated questions or statements. You can underline or put a bracket around each set to see the separation in the text.

What are some of the repeated phrases you found?

"Let them praise the name of the Lord, For He commanded and they were created." - Psalm 148:5

Thoughts to Surrender

Prayer for Others

_____

_____

_____

_____

_____

_____

_____

_____

_____

_____

_____

_____

_____

_____

_____

_____

_____

_____

_____

_____

_____

_____

_____

_____

_____

_____

Day Five

Today in Psalm 56 we are going to make observations. This could also be in the form of lists in the text. When he talks about what they (the enemy) wanted to do to him it is always followed by what they have done or are trying to do. I put circles around each of these in the list. There is also a small list of what God does or will do for him. Make a list of all of these.

What are the lists you found? Any other observations?

"O Lord, our Lord, How majestic is Your name in all the earth, Who have displayed Your splendor above the heavens! "
- Psalm 8:1

Thoughts to Surrender

Prayer for Yourself

Day Six

This is the last day in Psalm 56! Read it one more time. Make application to your own life from the observations you found. Did you notice things that you could start adding to your prayer life or focusing on more each day? Think about the focus of David as he wrote this Psalm in fear and in suffering.

What do you want to start adding to your prayers and daily walk to grow closer to God?

"Sing praise to the Lord, you His godly ones, And give thanks to His holy name." - Psalm 30:4

Thoughts to Surrender

Prayer for Others

Day Seven

Find a quote that you really like or has stuck out to you lately. It can be encouraging, inspirational, spiritual, anything that you need at this time. Write the quote here and if you're artsy, have fun with it!

Thoughts to Surrender

Prayer for Yourself

Week Four
Day One

And He has said to me, "My grace is sufficient for you, for power is perfected in weakness."
- 2 Corinthians 12:9

There is so much to learn from Paul in 2 Corinthians. We already went over a little bit of the background the other week, so we won't do that again. Instead we are going to talk more about Paul's suffering.

In 2 Corinthians 12:7-10, we learn that Paul was given a thorn in the flesh because God knew he would be prone to arrogance for having the revelations he had concerning Jesus and the gospel.

In verse 7b, "Because of the surpassing greatness of the revelations, for this reason, to keep me from exalting myself, there was given me a thorn in the flesh, a messenger of Satan to torment me—to keep me from exalting myself."

What did he mean by a messenger of Satan to torment him? Well, it's no surprise that Satan intends for his torment to be evil, but God's intention is for the good of the person enduring the suffering. God wants Paul to be made a better person through his suffering. If you remember our lesson from James 1, we talked about the motives behind our prayers. This is a great time to ask God how you can be made better through what you're suffering.

"Concerning this I implored the Lord three times that it might leave me." - 2 Corinthians 12:9

Paul begged to have this thorn in the flesh removed. We all know of someone else who begged for their suffering to be removed: Jesus.

Jesus knew what was going to happen. When He was in the garden, He begged God three times to take the suffering away. It was no secret that crucifixion was one of the slowest and most painful ways to die. When Jesus did not get an answer, or at least the answer He prayed for, He showed us how we need to respond to the "thorns in the flesh" we face in our lives, too. We need to respond the same way Jesus did in

Luke 22:42, "Father, if You are willing, remove this cup from Me; yet not My will, but Yours be done."

We have to remember that the suffering we face on earth is only temporary pain. There is a life with Christ later on that is far more beautiful than having everything we ask for on earth. Jesus knew what was waiting for Him when He finished His work on earth, but that didn't take away His suffering. He accepted His Father's answer knowing what He was brought here to do. We may not understand the pain we feel at the moment, and we may never get an answer for the pain in our lives, but I can promise you that remaining faithful and trusting God through every step will only make you stronger. Sometimes we have to accept the pain like Jesus did so we can keep going, knowing that we can one day help others through their pain by sharing our experience with them.

2 Corinthians 12:10, "Therefore I am well content with weaknesses, with insults, with distresses, with persecutions, with difficulties, for Christ's sake; for when I am weak, then I am strong."

Have you ever been so confident in something that it made you feel empowered with knowledge of the matter? Paul had this same confidence in the gospel of Jesus Christ.

We always say that God uses unlikely people for His work. The truth is, if we fully trust Him and do His will then the power of the gospel will work through us in ways we never knew were possible. We can have the confidence Paul had in his trials, knowing that God was on his side no matter what. He trusted God more than himself and we should too.

In Ephesians 6:10, "finally, be strong in the Lord and the strength of his might." Trust in the Lord more than yourself and God will use you in a powerful way. Paul demonstrates this in Acts 14:26 and Philippians 2. He trusted God in everything he did. God gave him the confidence to preach the gospel to people who could have had him killed. He never gave himself the credit, but always gave God the credit for what he had done.

FIND STRENGTH IN GOD AND CONFIDENCE THROUGH THE GOSPEL TO KEEP GOING!

Thoughts to Surrender

_____

_____

_____

_____

_____

_____

_____

_____

_____

_____

_____

_____

_____

_____

_____

_____

_____

_____

_____

_____

_____

Prayer for Others

Day Two

It's a new week and a new passage! Today, read through and look for words that are found more than once and are significant to the text, such as Lord, He, nations, earth, praise, trust, I, you, they, man, etc. Feel free to color these words with colored pencils or put boxes around them.

"God is our refuge and strength, A very present help in trouble Therefore we will not fear, though the earth should change And though the mountains slip into the heart of the sea; Though its waters roar and foam, Though the mountains quake at its swelling pride. There is a river whose streams make glad the city of God, The holy dwelling places of the Most High. God is in the midst of her, she will not be moved; God will help her when morning dawns. The nations made an uproar, the kingdoms tottered; He raised His voice, the earth melted. The Lord of hosts is with us; The God of Jacob is our stronghold. Come, behold the works of the Lord, Who has wrought desolations in the earth. He makes wars to cease to the end of the earth; He breaks the bow and cuts the spear in two; He burns the chariots with fire. "Cease striving and know that I am God; I will be exalted among the nations, I will be exalted in the earth." The Lord of hosts is with us; The God of Jacob is our stronghold."
- Psalm 46

What are your observations from the text so far? How many of each recurring word did you find?

"Open my eyes, that I may behold wonderful things from Your law."
- Psalm 119:18

Thoughts to Surrender

Prayer for Yourself

Day Three

Did you find any repeated phrases as you read through our Psalm for this week? What were they? Don't forget to underline them as you find them so you can see clear breaks in the text.

Thoughts to Surrender

Prayer for Others

Day Four

When you looked for repeated words, you may have noticed that the word earth was repeated several times. When looking at those repeated words it's important to see what they are connected to. Here we see a list of God being connected to things of the earth. What list you can find that shows God's power through the earth?

"Oh come, let us sing to the Lord; let us make a joyful noise to the rock of our salvation!" - Psalm 95:1

Thoughts to Surrender

Prayer for Yourself

Day Five

Now that you have broken down the text, let's break it up into sections. This is where your colored keywords really help out, along with your underlined phrases. Did you notice a pattern? Are they clustered in one area more than another? Do you see where you can connect verses to other verses based on the keywords?

For example, verses 1, 7, 11 are connected because they all indicate trust. I would put a bracket around the verse numbers and label to the side of each verse "their trust." To be super complicated, I like to color code each of the bracketed sections.

"Let the word of Christ dwell in you richly, teaching and admonishing one another in all wisdom." - Colossians 3:16

Thoughts to Surrender

Prayer for Others

Day Six

The fun part! Application for us today! We learn they were in chaos. Are we ever in chaos? How did they handle the chaos? How can we also handle our chaos in the same way? How can we let God be exalted in the trials?

"Let my lips utter praise, For You teach me Your statutes."
- Psalm 119:171

Thoughts to Surrender

Prayer for Yourself

_____
_____
_____
_____
_____
_____
_____
_____
_____
_____
_____
_____
_____
_____
_____
_____
_____
_____
_____
_____
_____
_____
_____
_____
_____
_____
_____
_____

Day Seven

Find a quote that you really like or has stuck out to you lately. It can be encouraging, inspirational, spiritual, anything that you need at this time. Write the quote out here and if you're artsy, have fun with it!

Thoughts to Surrender

Prayer for Others

Week Five
Day One

"But I want you to know, brethren, that the things which happened to me have actually turned out for the furtherance of the gospel." - Philippians 1:12

I love Paul because he saw so much suffering and trials yet continued to press on to the goal of advancing the gospel to as many people as he could reach. Paul was a great example to the church at Philippi, even though he was imprisoned. Philippi was a Roman colony with a very diverse culture. Nero was emperor of Rome at the time and was responsible for persecuting the church a year after Philippians was written.

Even though his letter was not about the persecution they were about to face, Paul still shared the kind of mindset he had through suffering. He pleads with the church to stay united through their difficult time. Two Christian sisters, Euodia and Syntyche, were fighting because they weren't unified.

We are going to take a look at how Paul used his suffering for good and how we can turn our suffering into something greater, too.

> **When you go through suffering and trials, how do you react to those circumstances?**
> _____
> _____
> _____
> _____

Starting in Philippians 1:7, "For it is only right for me to feel this way about you all, because I have you in my heart, since both in my imprisonment and in the defense and confirmation of the gospel, you all are partakers of grace with me."

Starting out, Paul lets them know that they are partakers of grace with him. He also lets them see that his heart is still thinking about and concerned for them while in prison, still defending and affirming the gospel.

In 1:9-11, we are given the theme to Philippians by his prayer for them.

Then in 1:12, 13 he gives his purpose statement, "Now I want you to know, brethren, that my circumstances have turned out for the greater progress of the gospel, so that my imprisonment in the cause of Christ has become well known throughout the whole praetorian guard and to everyone else,"

Even though Paul was suffering in prison, he found a way to make the best of his circumstance. He made it a point to be Christ-minded, which helped convert Roman soldiers through his faith and reaction to suffering.

Verses 1:15-18 are about two different types of preachers with different motives.

Moving forward to 1:19-26, we get the answer as to why. Why has Paul found confidence in his imprisonment? The answer is found here, because in these verses Paul said that he would magnify Christ in every way, whether through life or death. If he survived imprisonment, he would use his time to spread the gospel. If he died preaching Christ, his death would magnify Christ. His goal was to honor and live for Christ and make progress in the gospel.

When we spread the gospel, we put others before self and the gospel before self. How do we go about doing this when we are in a trial of our own?

In 1:27-30 Paul gives us the application the chapter. Here's what to do as Christians facing any sort of trial.

> **"Only let your manner of life be worthy of the gospel of Christ, so that whether I come and see you or am absent, I may hear of you that you are standing firm in one spirit, with one mind striving side by side for the faith of the gospel, and not frightened in anything by your opponents. This is a clear sign to them of their destruction, but of your salvation, and that from God. For it has been granted to you that for the sake of Christ you should not only believe in him but also suffer for his sake, engaged in the same conflict that you saw I had and now hear that I still have." - Philippians 1:27-30**

Our goal as Christians and citizens of Christ is to be of one mind, striving to further the gospel. The gospel is the message of Jesus, who unselfishly gave himself up so everyone can have hope of an eternity with Him. Does our behavior through good and bad times reflect Him, rather than our own selfish desires?

Be a Christian who isn't defeated by trials. Excel through the trial by putting others above yourself. Imitate Paul as he tried to imitate Christ's selflessness, meeting the needs of the souls around him before his own, despite the struggles he faced in a Roman prison.

It sounds like a lot to ask the moment a tragedy occurs, but I'm here to tell you that I've been there. I know your pain and I know it can be overcome, but it takes work and effort and I am praying for you. The reward of putting others above your trial is so uplifting to your walk with Christ, and it leads you to a deeper maturity in Christ. You can help others facing trials similar to your own.

Name three things you can do today to put others above yourself.

Grief Facts from Dr. H. Norman Wright:

The fourth and final phase of a crisis is the reconstruction phase, continued.

The crisis you experience gives you the chance to gain new strengths and perspectives on life. It gives you new values and changes how you approach life. (Wright, pg. 155)

Thoughts to Surrender

Prayer for Yourself

Day Two

We are in week five of going through different texts. By now you're a pro, right? Just as before, read through the passage one, two, or three times and really think about what the writer is saying. Look for repeated or significant words. Feel free to color these words with colored pencils or put boxes around them.

"Hear my prayer, O Lord, Give ear to my supplications! Answer me in Your faithfulness, in Your righteousness! And do not enter into judgment with Your servant, For in Your sight no man living is righteous. For the enemy has persecuted my soul; He has crushed my life to the ground; He has made me dwell in dark places, like those who have long been dead. Therefore my spirit is overwhelmed within me; My heart is appalled within me. I remember the days of old; I meditate on all Your doings; I muse on the work of Your hands. I stretch out my hands to You; My soul longs for You, as a parched land. Selah. Answer me quickly, O Lord, my spirit fails; Do not hide Your face from me, Or I will become like those who go down to the pit. Let me hear Your lovingkindness in the morning; For I trust in You; Teach me the way in which I should walk; For to You I lift up my soul. Deliver me, O Lord, from my enemies; I take refuge in You. Teach me to do Your will, For You are my God; Let Your good Spirit lead me on level ground. For the sake of Your name, O Lord, revive me. In Your righteousness bring my soul out of trouble. And in Your lovingkindness, cut off my enemies And destroy all those who afflict my soul, For I am Your servant." - Psalm 143

What are your observations from the text so far? How many of each recurring word did you find?

"Open my eyes, that I may behold the wonderful things of Your law." - Psalm 119:18

Thoughts to Surrender

Prayer for Others

Day Three

    Did you find any repeated phrases as you read through our Psalm for this week? What were they? Don't forget to underline them as you find them so you can see clear breaks in the text. Are you already seeing any breaks in the text?

" **Therefore let us be grateful for receiving a kingdom that cannot be shaken, and thus let us offer to God acceptable worship, with reverence and awe." - Hebrews 12:28**

Thoughts to Surrender

Prayer for Yourself

Day Four

When looking at those repeated words, it's important to see what they're connected to. The first set of repeated words describe who God is. David prays to God in his time of affliction, but he makes known to God that he has not forgotten who He is. What lists or patterns have you noticed that show who God is?

Then take a moment to look for a list of things that David asks of God. Finding these lists help with application to our own lives and an understanding of the text.

"Because Your steadfast love is better than life, my lips will praise You." - Psalm 63:3

Thoughts to Surrender

Prayer for Others

Day Five

    We're continuing our search for lists within the text. What can you find that shows David's thoughts on God?

    Example: I trust in You.

    Start thinking of how these lists could help you when you're feeling despair. What are some things you can relate to? What do you see that you might need to change in your own prayers on those hard days when you compare your troubles to David's?

"I will give thanks to the Lord with my whole heart; I will recount all of Your wonderful deeds." - Psalm 9:1

Thoughts to Surrender

Prayer for Yourself

Day Six

There is still so much to be found in this text, so I want to encourage you to keep searching for things, like breaking it into sections or finding verses that connect to each other. See if there is a main verse that makes David's point clear.

While you search the text, focus on application to be found. We know David was in affliction. He spent a great deal of time literally on the run from Saul and his men. Even though we aren't experiencing the same afflictions as David, we can still have heartache that sounds like David's plea to God.

What are things you notice that could be similar to your own prayers compared to David's? What do you notice that you might need to change in your prayers?

Thoughts to Surrender

Prayer for Others

Day Seven

Find a quote that you really like or has stuck out to you lately. It can be encouraging, inspirational, spiritual, anything that you need at this time. Write the quote here and if you're artsy, have fun with it!

Thoughts to Surrender

Prayer for Yourself

Week Six
Day One

"And who is he who will harm you if you become followers of what is good?" - 1 Peter 3:13

Peter was an apostle who witnessed Christ's sufferings firsthand, something few could claim. He also experienced a lot of suffering alongside other faithful Christians due to Neronian persecution. Even though Peter was going through the same trials as others around him, there was something he continued to do he encouraged them to hang onto their salvation (5:12). He wanted them to never give up even though they had to suffer for a while. They had an inheritance waiting for them in heaven if they could just stand firm in their trust.

This is the message that rings throughout the book of 1 Peter. Finding great joy in suffering for doing good instead of evil gives us hope because we will have glory in the end.

In America, we don't suffer the same way early Christians did, but we can still hold onto our hope of salvation. We can find joy in our suffering.

"Who is there to harm you if you prove zealous for what is good? But even if you should suffer for the sake of righteousness, you are blessed. And do not fear their intimidation, and do not be troubled"
- 1 Peter 3:13, 14

You have to change your mindset, wanting to do good so badly that no one can get close to taking your salvation. You have no reason to be afraid of those who cause your trials. We are to fear God more than people. God gives us our hope of salvation, and He alone can take it away.

"but sanctify Christ as Lord in your hearts, always being ready to make a defense to everyone who asks you to give an account for the hope that is in you, yet with gentleness and reverence; and keep a good conscience so that in the thing in which you are slandered, those who revile your good behavior in Christ will be put to shame. For it is better, if God should will it so, that you suffer for doing what is right rather than for doing what is wrong." - 1 Peter 3:15-17

I've already mentioned that we have the ability to change our circumstances, and this is what I mean by that. When we try to do good while going through trials, we are more capable of defending our hope. Apologia means "to make a defense" in Koine Greek. We can use our suffering as a way to evangelize to others. Trying to do good for others will sometimes be met with resistance. Don't pay any attention to those people who are out to destroy your hope. They don't know why you're doing what you're doing, but one day the gospel might prick their hearts because of something you say or do during your own suffering. If they never change their hearts, they will, sadly, be put to shame at judgment. We are far better off suffering at the hands of man than the hands of God in the end. So, dear sisters, HOLD ON TO YOUR SALVATION. Do not let anyone try to take this hope away from you. It's far more precious than anything in this world.

"For Christ also died for sins once for all, the just for the unjust, so that He might bring us to God, having been put to death in the flesh, but made alive in the spirit." - 1 Peter 3:18

So, this verse explains 15-17. It's why we sanctify Christ as Lord in our hearts and why we're always ready to defend our hope. Christ died once for all so that He might bring us to God. This is why we are willing to suffer.

"in which also He went and made proclamation to the spirits now in prison, who once were disobedient, when the patience of God kept waiting in the days of Noah, during the construction of the ark, in which a few, that is, eight persons, were brought safely through the water." - 1 Peter 3:19, 20

Noah preached to the disobedient during his time. He preached for 120 years while building the ark. The only people saved were Noah's family. Jesus also preached to the disobedient Jews before gospel went out to the gentiles. The mission or goal was the same: to bring us to God.

"Corresponding to that, baptism now saves you—not the removal of dirt from the flesh, but an appeal to God for a good conscience— through the resurrection of Jesus Christ." - 1 Peter 3:21

Only eight souls were saved in Noah's time. Jesus came to save us all! We have an amazing message to share with others so that they can be saved and understand why we have so much hope. They can understand why we try to be good to those who hurt us or do good when we have days of doubt and depression. We have to keep pushing forward because of our goal to be with God one day.

Many don't realize that baptism by immersion was not something new the apostles started. The Jews had immersion pools outside of every temple so that those coming to worship could go into the baptismal pool and out the other side, cleansed before entering worship. So, for Christians our rebirth can only come through immersion.

We go through all of that because of 1 Peter 4:1, "Therefore, since Christ has suffered in the flesh, arm yourselves also with the same purpose, because he who has suffered in the flesh has ceased from sin,"

When we see a "therefore," we need to investigate what came before it. This is basically a summary of 3:18. Bringing glory to God is a constantly repeated theme in this book. When we seek to have the same purpose as Christ while we're in this body, we are ultimately are striving to remove sin from our lives and live in a way that pleases God and brings Him glory. That's through the struggles we face, through our good times, and through and through our behavior every day. If you're doing this study in a time of grief, keep this in mind. We are no longer tempted to sin when we suffer for doing what is right in God's eyes. You're ultimately stopping the influence of sin in your life when you allow yourself to suffer.

Jumping a few verses ahead

"Whoever speaks, is to do so as one who is speaking the utterances of God; whoever serves is to do so as one who is serving by the strength which God supplies; so that in all things God may be glorified through Jesus Christ, to whom belongs the glory and dominion forever and ever. Amen. Beloved, do not be surprised at the fiery ordeal among you, which comes upon you for your testing, as though some strange thing were happening to you; but to the degree that you share the sufferings of Christ, keep on rejoicing, so that also at the revelation of His glory you may rejoice with exultation. If you are reviled for the name of Christ, you are blessed, because the Spirit of glory and of God rests on you." - 1 Peter 4:11-14,

In 4:11, when we speak to or serve others we need to glorify God through our actions. We should always be focused on God. If we turn our suffering around to bring glory to God, we will have a bigger impact on others. It will impact their view of us because of how we handle ourselves while suffering. Our behavior is a witness or testimony to others. In 4:12, don't think of your suffering as something strange, even though our grief may be caused by an unexpected tragedy.

In the context of 1 Peter, the fiery ordeal that Christians were facing was caused by Nero. He was burning Christians in the streets, using them as lamps in the middle of the night. They were going through intense situations and had great fears. The message Peter gave them was to change their focus from physical suffering to eternal hope if they suffered for doing right. Trials test our faith. They test our willingness to stand fast in the gospel, anticipating the eternity waiting for us. Stay true to Christ through your grief and pain.

Then in 4:13 and 14, hope is found. We share Christ's suffering when we suffer. We can truly rejoice knowing that we are in fellowship with Christ. We have to find some joy in suffering; if this is the only thing you can find, so be it. If we choose Christ over the world, others' opinions, or hateful answers to what we're experiencing, we are blessed. I would rather seek God's approval than the world's approval.

When we experience grief, people often give advice that isn't spiritually uplifting or pleasing to God. They might tell you what you don't want to hear or what they think is right, but this usually hurts more than it helps. Seek God's will in overcoming the trial through your own prayers, through serving others, and by how you live each day. It won't take away the pain, but staying close to God through your trials will give you peace in the long run. We learn more from our suffering this way. We build endurance and the ability to help others.

Thoughts to Surrender

Prayer for Others

Day Two

We are down to our last lesson on breaking down text. By now you're a pro, right? Just as before, read the passage all the way through one, two or three times and really think about what the writer is saying. Look for repeated or significant words. Feel free to color these words with colored pencils or put boxes around them.

"The Lord reigns, let the earth rejoice; Let the many islands be glad. Clouds and thick darkness surround Him; Righteousness and justice are the foundation of His throne. Fire goes before Him And burns up His adversaries round about. His lightnings lit up the world; The earth saw and trembled. The mountains melted like wax at the presence of the Lord, At the presence of the Lord of the whole earth. The heavens declare His righteousness, And all the peoples have seen His glory. Let all those be ashamed who serve graven images, Who boast themselves of idols; Worship Him, all you gods. Zion heard this and was glad, And the daughters of Judah have rejoiced Because of Your judgments, O Lord. For You are the Lord Most High over all the earth; You are exalted far above all gods. Hate evil, you who love the Lord, Who preserves the souls of His godly ones; He delivers them from the hand of the wicked. Light is sown like seed for the righteous And gladness for the upright in heart. Be glad in the Lord, you righteous ones, And give thanks to His holy name."
- Psalm 97

What are your observations from the text so far? How many of each recurring word did you find?

"In everything give thanks; for this is God's will for you in Christ Jesus" - 1 Thessalonians 5:18

Thoughts to Surrender

Prayer for Yourself

Day Three

Do you see any breaks in the text?

They could be a change in thought, like a complaint or praise, different sets of people the author is talking about, or even objects or comparisons.

"But his delight is in the law of the Lord, And in His law he meditates day and night." - Psalm 1:2

Thoughts to Surrender

Prayer for Others

Day Four

When you look at breaks in the text, do you notice any particular groups of people or objects that are emphasized in each break? These different groups can be connected through a keyword: rejoice.

Ask yourself while you're through the text and find recurring words like rejoice. Who or what is rejoicing?

"Let not the oppressed return dishonored; Let the afflicted and needy praise Your name." - Psalm 74:21

Thoughts to Surrender

Prayer for Yourself

Day Five

Let's make some lists! You may have noticed in the first section that there are several characteristics of God. Those attributes can be listed.

We just talked about the word rejoice. Who or what was rejoicing and why? Make a list that explains who rejoices here.

"The eyes of the Lord are toward the righteous and his ears toward their cry" - Psalm 34:15

Thoughts to Surrender

Prayer for Others

_____

_____

_____

_____

_____

_____

_____

_____

_____

_____

_____

_____

_____

_____

_____

_____

_____

_____

_____

_____

_____

_____

_____

_____

_____

_____

_____

Day Six

Through these lists we are able to see how God reigns in each of the groups, and what they were rejoicing about.

We can rejoice about a lot of the same things they did! What are some things the saints and Judah rejoiced about that you can rejoice about, too?

Thoughts to Surrender

Prayer for Yourself

Day Seven

Find a quote that you really like or that has stuck out to you lately.
It can be encouraging, inspirational, spiritual, anything that you need at
this time. Write the quote out here, and if you're artsy, have fun with it!

Thoughts to Surrender

Prayer for Others

Week Seven
Day One

"When the righteous cry out for help, the Lord hears and delivers them out of all their troubles. The Lord is near to the brokenhearted and saves the crushed in spirit." - Psalm 34:17, 18

This journey of grief is very different for everyone. We have different crises that hit our lives and they affect each of us differently. My own grief was a variety of things. They came at different ages, different stages of life, and different stages of my walk with God. I experienced my parent's divorce, the loss of my grandparents, cousins and friends, and a miscarriage in my first year of marriage. Then came the loss of my brother, which was by far the hardest crisis of them all for me.

What I can promise you is that the grief crisis will not last forever. They are only here for a short time. The way we choose to handle ourselves during crisis and grief will make a huge impact on how we overcome.

For me, grief was not easy. I experienced every phase of grief described in Dr. H. Norman Wright's book. I felt that 2x4 to the face and heart the moment I found out about my brother. I experienced the need to find every photo, to hold onto every memory we had together. I, too, begged God to take every bit of grace He was going to offer me as His child and give it to my brother instead. The truth is that grief is hard. It hurts. It takes time to heal and grow into a new life after the initial impact.

Never ignore your hurt and feelings. It's okay to cry and let your feelings out when you need to. I strongly advise having a close friend who is willing to listen. I was fortunate to have several friends who had experienced my trial. They provided a lot of insight and help for months after it happened. It's also OKAY to know when you need to see a professional. I went to an amazing grief therapist for a long time after I lost my brother. She provided so much guidance on how to handle grief in a healthy way, so that I wouldn't fall into depression.

From here on I want to encourage you to do the following:

- Continue journaling if it has become a place of peace and comfort for you.
- Continue searching for someone else in need that you can be a blessing to.
- If you're still in a lot of pain and need further guidance, please contact your local minister and see if they can help. Or, contact a professional counselor to help guide you through these confusing times.
- Keep finding passages to break down. Whether it's going through all of the Psalms or a section of text from the New Testament, you can keep the fun of breaking down the text going!

Thoughts to Surrender

_____

_____

_____

_____

_____

_____

_____

_____

_____

_____

_____

_____

_____

_____

_____

_____

_____

Prayer for Yourself

Resources

- Wright, H. Norman. *The Complete Guide to Crisis & Trauma Counseling*: What to Do and Say When It Matters Most! Bethany House Publishers, 2011.

Lightning Source UK Ltd.
Milton Keynes UK
UKHW02142580122
397823UK00006B/147